ARISE, WOMAN OF LIGHT
The Prophetic Awakening of Daughters and Nations

by Dr. Prophetess Racheal Odoy

"When one woman rises in her light, nations follow."

Giant Publishing Company
Lincoln, Nebraska USA

Copyright 2025 Dr. Prophetess Racheal Odoy

Published by Giant Publishing Company
Post Office Box 6455
Lincoln, NE 68506
www.giantpublishingcompany.com

Printed in the United States of America.

All rights reserved. No part of this publication may be used or reproduced in any form or by any means, electronic or mechanical, including photocopying, recording, or by any information storage and retrieval system, without prior written permission from the author, except for brief quotations used in reviews or articles.

Scripture quotations are from the King James Version (KJV) of the Holy Bible, used with acknowledgment.

ISBN: 979-8-9898098-2-0

Odoy, Racheal
Arise, Woman of Light
Non-fiction/Racheal Odoy
1. Non-fiction-Christianity
2. Bible commentary
3. Self-help

Cover design: Dr. Prophetess Racheal Odoy

Also by Dr. Prophetess Racheal Odoy:

You Need a Jonathan
Copyright 2018

I and My Seed will Thrive
Copyright 2019

You Have No Carbon Copy
Copyright 2020

Dedication

To my beloved husband,
Apostle Dr. Larry Odoy,
my greatest encourager and pillar of strength.
Your steadfast love, faith, and support have carried me
through every stage of this writing journey.
You have stood beside me with patience and prayer,
reminding me that vision thrives
where there are unity and divine partnership.

To my precious children, my priceless gifts from God,
what a joy it has been to have you near
as I wrote under the leading of the Holy Spirit.
Your laughter, presence, and gentle hearts
have never been a distraction,
but a sweet reminder of God's faithfulness
and blessing in our home.

And to our faithful ministry partners and intercessors,
who continually lift us in prayer
and stand with us in the work of the Kingdom
this book is also yours.
Your dedication, intercession, and sacrifice
have been a fragrance before God,
and through you, the light of this ministry shines brighter.

To each of you, with love and gratitude
may God reward your labor abundantly.

Acknowledgments

I thank the Lord who has been my strength, my inspiration, and my voice in every season of life.

To every woman who dares to believe that **God still speaks at midnight and where you are**, this book is for you.

To every reader, intercessor, and woman walking through her own season of rising, this book is for you.

May these words remind you that God still speaks, still heals, and still raises women of light.

Preface

"Arise, shine; for thy light is come, and the glory of the LORD is risen upon thee." Isaiah 60 : 1 (KJV)

There are seasons when God seems silent, and yet He is speaking louder than ever - speaking through stillness, through tears, through the breaking. It was in such a midnight hour that the Spirit of the Lord whispered to me: **"Arise."**

Those five letters carried resurrection. They carried a commission. They carried the weight of nations hidden inside a woman's obedience.

This book was birthed in one of the darkest seasons of my life - a season when I thought everything had ended. But at **midnight**, when pain had become my closest companion, the Lord spoke clearly:

"Arise, for when you arise, other women will rise."

Those words became the spark that ignited *Arise, Woman of Light*.

This book is more than inspiration; it is an *awakening* - a call to every woman who has been silenced, broken, or overlooked.

It is a reminder that your **pain can become power**, your **wounds can become wisdom**, and your **story can become someone else's light**.

May every chapter wash over your heart like morning light. May every verse awaken faith you thought was lost.

May your tears turn into oil. May your voice echo across generations. And may you discover that you were never forgotten - only being prepared.

Author's Note

When I began to write, I didn't write from comfort, I wrote from **healing**.

I wrote from the ashes of betrayal, from the wilderness of waiting, and from the altars of midnight prayers.

Many times, I asked God, *"Why me?"* And His answer was simple:

"Because when you rise, others will find courage to rise too."

This book carries that prophetic wind - a mantle of awakening.

Every story, every scripture, and every declaration within these pages was birthed through prayer and revelation.

If you are holding this book, know this: Heaven has called you by name.

You are not forgotten. You are not finished. You are a **woman of light** and the world is waiting for your glow.

Table of Contents, page 1

Chapter 1	The Woman Who Heard "Arise"	Page 1
Chapter 2	You are a Nation Within a Woman	Page 5
Chapter 3	From Darkness to Dawning	Page 9
Chapter 4	The Power of a Spoken Word	Page 13
Chapter 5	The Woman Who Builds Her House	Page 17
Chapter 6	When Faith Feels Empty	Page 21
Chapter 7	The Oil of Endurance	Page 25
Chapter 8	The Woman Who Sees Beyond the Storm	Page 29
Chapter 9	When the Alabaster Breaks	Page 35
Chapter 10	The Silent Battles of a Strong Woman	Page 39

Table of Contents, page 2

Chapter 11	When Destiny Demands Separation	Page 43
Chapter 12	The Power of Forgiveness	Page 49
Chapter 13	Love That Learns: When Betrayal Becomes a Teacher	Page 53
Chapter 14	The Rise of the Deborah Generation	Page 59
Chapter 15	The Power of a Prophetic Woman's Voice	Page 65
Chapter 16	The Woman and the Seed	Page 71
Chapter 17	When Pain Becomes a Platform	Page 77
Chapter 18	You Are a Nation	Page 85
Chapter 19	Arise and Shine	Page 91
Closing Blessing	A Word to Every Daughter Who Reads This Book	Page 98
About the Author		Page 101

She Who Arises

By Dr. Prophetess Racheal Odoy

She once hid behind the shadows of her own doubt,
measuring her worth by the voices that wounded her.
Her mirror spoke fear, her heart whispered "not enough,"
and her dreams faded beneath the dust of yesterday.

But Heaven waited.
The voice of the Lord broke through her midnight
"Daughter, throw off the old mantle,
the one of fear, failure, and forgotten faith.
Take up your light again."

She trembled, yet she obeyed.
With shaking hands, she lifted the flame,
and what once looked small began to glow.
It starts with you, but it's never about you
for your light births courage in others.

She who once wept now wipes her tears.
She who once feared now walks on water.

Every scar becomes oil, every sigh a song.
She is clothed in strength and crowned with mercy,
her past now the perfume of grace.

Arise, woman of light.
Your voice is no longer a whisper
it is a trumpet to the nations.
Your steps ignite trails for others to follow.
For you are no longer hidden;
you are His reflection in motion,
the dawn after the long night.

"Arise, shine; for thy light is come, and the glory of the LORD is risen upon thee." **Isaiah 60 : 1 (KJV)**

Chapter 1

The Woman Who Heard "Arise"

When God's Whisper Becomes Your Turning Point

"Fear not: for I have redeemed thee, I have called thee by thy name; thou art mine." **Isaiah 43 : 1 (KJV)**

There comes a night when every light seems to fade, when the silence grows so heavy that it presses on your chest, and you wonder if Heaven still remembers your name. I had known that kind of night. A night when faith feels like a forgotten language, when you pray but your words echo back like whispers in an empty room.

Yet it was in that very silence that I heard Him. Not in thunder, not in fire, but in the still small voice that pierces every wall of despair.

The voice of the Lord came softly, but with a power that no circumstance could resist: **"Arise."**

That single word was life. It wasn't an invitation; it was a command. Heaven was not asking me if I felt ready to rise; it was declaring that *I had already been chosen* to rise.

At that moment, I understood that when God says *Arise*, He is not speaking to your body; He is speaking to your destiny. He is commanding everything dormant in you - your vision, your faith, your joy - to awaken.

For months I had been asking God, "Why me? Why this wilderness?" I thought I had lost everything that defined me: people I trusted, plans I built, dreams I carried since childhood. But the Lord began to show me that **every breaking carries a birthing**. He was not ending my story; He was rewriting it in His own ink.

"Arise from the dust, O Jerusalem; sit enthroned…" **Isaiah 52:2 (KJV)**

You cannot sit in ashes when God has called you to shine. You cannot keep mourning when Heaven has assigned you to move nations. When God whispers *Arise*, it means He has already placed within you the strength to stand. You don't rise because you feel strong; you rise because His word ignites strength in you.

That word *Arise* will confront your comfort. It will shake you out of places you've been hiding. It will demand faith when fear seems more familiar. But it's in that shaking that transformation begins.

I remember praying one night, "Lord, I don't even know how to begin again."

He said, "You don't need to begin again; you need to *get up* and I will carry you."

Each time you obey the call to arise, you give God permission to make your pain prophetic. Your tears become seeds. Your story becomes a mirror through which other women can see hope.

You may not feel qualified, but Heaven's call is never based on your qualifications; it's anchored in your *calling*. And every calling begins with a simple act of obedience - standing up - when everything in you wants to stay down.

So, woman of God, let this be your moment. Shake off the heaviness. Speak to your spirit. Say to your heart, *"I will arise."* Because when one woman rises in light, generations behind her find their way home.

For Reflection

1. When has God's whisper interrupted your silence?
2. What areas of your life is He commanding to rise again today?

Prophetic Declarations

• I arise from every season of defeat and walk boldly in divine purpose.
• My past no longer defines me; the voice of God directs me.
• My light will not be dimmed; my destiny will not be delayed.

Prayer

Father, thank You for calling me by name. Even in the night, Your voice awakens my soul. Teach me to rise with strength, to stand with faith, and to shine for Your glory. Where I have been broken, breathe new life. Where I have been silent, put Your word in my mouth. I choose today to Arise, for Your glory has come. In Jesus' mighty name, Amen.

Chapter 2

You Are a Nation Within a Woman

Carrying Generations in Your Spirit

"And the LORD said unto her, Two nations are in thy womb, and two manner of people shall be separated from thy bowels." **Genesis 25 : 23 (KJV)**

Every woman carries more than breath; she carries destiny. Inside a woman's obedience lies the blueprint of generations. When God looks at a woman, He does not merely see her present form; He sees kingdoms, voices, and movements waiting to be born through her "Yes."

Rebekah's story reminds us that sometimes the war you feel within is not a sign of failure but of future. Two nations wrestled inside her, and the turmoil was God's way of announcing that what she carried was significant. The pain of the process did not disqualify her; it proved she was hosting promise.

So it is with every woman who has ever wondered, *"Why me? Why this weight?"* Heaven whispers back, *"Because nations are in you."* The warfare you face is evidence that what you carry threatens darkness. The enemy would not fight you so fiercely if your womb, natural or spiritual, were empty.

Some women carry songs; others carry businesses, ministries, reforms, or movements that will shift culture.

Yet all of us are carriers of divine purpose. Our wombs, both physical and spiritual, are sacred places where Heaven plants possibility.

"Before I formed thee in the belly I knew thee; and before thou camest forth out of the womb I sanctified thee." Jeremiah 1 : 5 (KJV)

Even before you knew who you were, God had already written what you would become. You are the answer to a problem that exists in the earth. Every assignment you've carried the child you nurtured, the idea you released, the prayer you prayed in secret was God expanding His Kingdom through you.

Sometimes the carrying feels lonely. Sometimes the stretching feels unbearable. But every mother of destiny learns that pain is part of birthing. Mary endured misunderstanding, Hannah endured delay, and yet both delivered what changed history. You are in good company.

Do not curse the contraction. The pressure is proof that delivery is near. The discomfort you feel is not punishment; it's prophecy in motion.

For Reflection

1. What vision, dream, or promise do you sense God forming inside you right now?
2. How can you protect and nurture what Heaven has entrusted to you while it matures?

Prophetic Declarations

- I am a carrier of nations, chosen to birth divine purpose.
- No warfare will silence what God has placed within me.
- My womb, spiritual and natural, is a sanctuary of destiny.

Prayer

Father, thank You for trusting me with what is holy. Teach me to carry promise with grace and guard it with wisdom. When I grow weary, remind me that nations wait on my obedience. Let the sound of my faith shake generations yet unborn. I yield to Your timing and Your process, and I declare that what You planted in me shall live. In Jesus' name, Amen.

Chapter 3

From Darkness to Dawning

When the Night Breaks Open With Light

"Weeping may endure for a night, but joy cometh in the morning."
Psalm 30 : 5 (KJV)

There are seasons when the darkness seems endless - when betrayal, disappointment, or loss covers every dream like a heavy curtain. In those moments you wonder if morning will ever come. Yet God, who separates light from darkness, never allows night to last forever. Every trial has an appointed sunrise.

I have learned that dawn does not begin with noise; it begins with a glimmer. God never waits for your circumstances to change before He calls the light to rise; He *commands* the light while it is still dark. He speaks into your midnight, *"Let there be light."*

When the Lord begins to bring you out, the shift is subtle. The heaviness lifts little by little. The same situations that once crushed you begin to reveal lessons instead of pain. The Spirit whispers, "You are coming out," and suddenly you realize that you are standing where you once wept.

Every woman who has ever walked through a night season knows this truth: **darkness is the womb of revelation**. It is in the night that God teaches you His voice, molds your faith, and trains your eyes to see the faint light of His promises.

Think of Ruth. She left Moab's darkness of loss and famine and followed the faint glow of purpose. She did not know that gleaning in a stranger's field would lead her to destiny. Or Mary Magdalene, who came to the tomb while it was still dark, only to become the first witness of the risen Lord. Light meets those who dare to move in the dark.

"The people that walked in darkness have seen a great light." Isaiah 9 : 2 (KJV)

Do not despise your night; it is training you for dawn. When the morning comes, you will not only rejoice, you will understand why the night was necessary.

For Reflection

1. What area of your life feels like night right now?
2. Can you identify small "glimmers" of God's light already appearing there?

Prophetic Declarations

• My night cannot hold me; I rise into divine morning.
• What was hidden in darkness will be revealed in light.
• My tears have watered the soil of my joy, and I will reap with singing.

Prayer

Father, thank You that You are faithful even in my darkest hours. Teach me to trust You when I cannot see the way. Let Your light break through my confusion, my fear, and my grief. As morning comes, let my life testify that You turn mourning into dancing and ashes into beauty.

In Jesus' name, Amen.

Chapter 4

The Power of a Spoken Word

Creating Life With the Tongue of Faith

"Death and life are in the power of the tongue: and they that love it shall eat the fruit thereof." **Proverbs 18 : 21 (KJV)**

Every word you speak is a seed. Heaven listens when you open your mouth. The same voice that once cried out in pain can become a trumpet of victory when it begins to agree with God's Word.

For years I spoke from my wounds, unaware that my tongue was painting my tomorrow. I said what I felt instead of what God said, and my atmosphere mirrored my emotions. But one day the Lord whispered, *"Daughter, if you will speak My promises, I will frame your world again."*

In the beginning, God did not build creation with His hands; He **spoke**. And when He said *"Let there be light,"* darkness had no choice but to obey. The same creative authority rests inside His daughters today. When you declare His Word, you are not merely reciting Scripture, you are legislating Heaven's will upon the earth.

"So shall My word be that goeth forth out of My mouth: it shall not return unto Me void." **Isaiah 55 : 11 (KJV)**

The Ten "God Said" Moments

In **Genesis chapter one**, the phrase *"And God said"* appears **ten times**. That's not coincidence; it's divine rhythm. Ten is the number of order and completion - a sign that creation itself came into alignment through the spoken Word of God.

Every time God "said," something shifted.

- *"And God said, Let there be light..."* and light came.
- *"And God said, Let the waters under the heaven be gathered..."* and they obeyed.
- *"And God said, Let the earth bring forth grass..."* and life sprang from dust.

With each declaration, creation stepped closer to fullness. The universe did not argue with His voice; it responded. The same creative force now resides in the tongue of every believer. When we speak God's Word, we echo His authority, bringing heaven's order into earthly chaos.

This is why the enemy fights to silence the prophetic woman. He knows that one Spirit-filled sentence from your mouth can alter the course of generations. When a woman of faith declares, *"Let there be peace in my home,"* or *"Let healing come to my body,"* those words do not fall to the ground, they begin to create.

We are made in the image of a speaking God. Your tongue is not merely for expression; it is for creation. The same God who spoke ten times in Genesis is still speaking through you today.

The enemy fears a woman who understands the authority of her voice. He wants you to believe that silence is safety, but silence can be bondage when God has given you a command to speak. Every declaration of truth dismantles lies. Every time you say, *"I shall live and not die,"* you release light into your atmosphere.

Remember the woman with the issue of blood said within herself, *"If I may but touch His garment, I shall be whole."* Her miracle began not with her hands, but with her words. Your confession directs your movement; your speech aligns your steps with destiny.

So, speak life over your children, your home, your vision, your ministry. Speak healing even when pain lingers. Speak prosperity even when provision seems far. You are not denying reality - you are declaring truth that transcends it.

For Reflection

1. Have your words lately built faith or fed fear?
2. What atmosphere are your declarations creating around you?

Prophetic Declarations

- My tongue is an instrument of life and restoration.
- I speak what God speaks, and creation responds.
- My voice carries authority; my words birth destiny.

Prayer

Father, place Your words in my mouth. Let every syllable that leaves my lips agree with Heaven. Teach me to bless when it would be easier to curse, to declare light when darkness presses in. May my speech become prophecy that builds, heals, and restores. In Jesus' mighty name, Amen.

Chapter 5

The Woman Who Builds Her House

Wisdom as the Foundation of Her Dwelling

"Every wise woman buildeth her house: but the foolish plucketh it down with her hands." **Proverbs 14 : 1 (KJV)**

A woman carries the blueprint of her home in her spirit. The atmosphere of a house, its peace, its stability, its love, flows from the heart of the woman within it. When Scripture says *"Every wise woman buildeth her house,"* it is not only speaking of bricks and wood; it is speaking of **spiritual architecture.**

To build your house means to establish order, prayer, and faith within every room of your life. A house is not truly built until wisdom holds the hammer. Without it, the strongest walls can crumble under the pressure of storms.

When the Lord spoke to me about this scripture, He said, *"You do not build with opinions, you build with principles. You do not construct with emotions, you build with understanding."* True wisdom comes from His Word, and when a woman builds on that foundation, her house becomes a fortress that cannot be shaken.

"Therefore whosoever heareth these sayings of mine, and doeth them, I will liken him unto a wise man, which built his house upon a rock." **Matthew 7 : 24 (KJV)**

Abigail: The Woman Who Stood Between Destruction and Destiny

The Bible gives us a portrait of such wisdom in **1 Samuel 25**. David had sent his young men to Nabal, a wealthy man in Carmel, requesting food for his soldiers. Nabal answered them harshly, scorning David and dishonoring the anointed one of God.

His foolish words triggered David's anger. The warrior who once spared Saul's life now rose in fury, ready to destroy Nabal and every man in his household before dawn. Judgment was on its way to Nabal's door.

But in that household was a woman named **Abigail** who was discerning, humble, and quick to act. The servants ran to her, saying, *"Evil is determined against our master and against all his household."* Without delay, she gathered food, wine, and provision and set out to meet David.

She did not consult her husband, for she understood that wisdom sometimes requires **silent obedience** and quick intervention. When Abigail met David, she bowed before him and spoke words soaked in humility and grace:

"Upon me, my lord, let this iniquity be." **1 Samuel 25 : 24 (KJV)**

Those words shifted the atmosphere. Her gentle speech disarmed a man ready for war. Her offering turned wrath into mercy. David's sword returned to its sheath because a woman **chose wisdom over pride**.

"Blessed be the Lord God of Israel, which sent thee this day to meet me: and blessed be thy advice, and blessed be thou." **1 Samuel 25 : 32–33 (KJV)**

Abigail did not only save her husband; she saved the entire household. Her discernment became the wall that protected her home. And later, when Nabal died, God elevated her. She became the wife of King David.

Beloved, a wise woman's decisions can redirect destiny. She doesn't just preserve her home; she positions it for divine favor. Like Abigail, she speaks peace when anger roars, she moves in humility when pride could destroy, and she covers her family in prayer when danger draws near.

A woman of wisdom is a bridge between destruction and deliverance. She doesn't build with fear; she builds with foresight. She doesn't respond with emotion; she responds with revelation.

When the storms of life come, and they will, it is the woman who builds on the Rock that will stand unbroken. She knows how to bend in the wind without breaking, because her foundation is not emotional, it's eternal.

Beloved, God is calling you to be the wise builder. He is calling you to lay every brick of your life on the foundation of His Word: your family, your ministry, your business, your destiny. Each act of obedience is a stone. Each prayer is cement. Each declaration is a beam of strength that holds your purpose together.

Let your home, both physical and spiritual, become a sanctuary where Heaven feels welcome.

For Reflection

1. How do you respond when crisis comes - through emotion or through wisdom?
2. What lessons can you draw from Abigail's actions to apply in your own home or ministry?

Prophetic Declarations

• I am a wise builder; my house is established in truth and peace.
• Like Abigail, I carry the spirit of discernment and divine timing.
• My wisdom disarms every plan of destruction against my family.

Prayer

Lord, make me a wise builder. Teach my heart to choose peace over pride, and my tongue to speak life over every wall of my house. Give me the wisdom of Abigail to act swiftly, humbly, and righteously. Let my presence bring calm where chaos threatens and light where darkness presses. May my life be a refuge that honors You. In Jesus' name, Amen.

Chapter 6

When Faith Feels Empty

Trusting God in the Silent Season

"Now faith is the substance of things hoped for, the evidence of things not seen." **Hebrews 11 : 1 (KJV)**

There are moments when faith feels like a distant echo when you've prayed every prayer, declared every promise, and still Heaven seems quiet. You fast, you sow, you wait, and yet no answer comes. You begin to ask, *"Lord, where are You? Have You forgotten me?"*

Every believer faces such a season. It is not proof that your faith has failed, it is proof that your faith is being refined. True faith is not measured by how loud we shout when everything is working; it is revealed by how steadfastly we stand when nothing seems to move.

I remember walking through such a season. My prayers felt heavy, my spirit weary. I could not feel God, yet I could not deny Him either. And in that silence, He whispered, *"I am teaching you to believe Me without needing to see Me."*

Faith is not a feeling, it is a position. You can't always trace God, but you can trust Him. Even when your hands are empty, your heart can still hold hope. The emptiness is not punishment, it is preparation. God empties vessels so He can fill them with something new.

"Blessed is she that believed: for there shall be a performance of those things which were told her from the Lord." **Luke 1 : 45 (KJV)**

When **Mary** received the word from the angel Gabriel in **Luke 1 : 26–38**, she had no visible sign, no proof - only a promise. Yet she believed. Her faith conceived before her body ever did. That is what God is teaching you to conceive with your spirit even when your situation looks barren.

This is just as it was for **Hannah** in **1 Samuel 1 : 9–20**. She went up to the temple, year after year, with tears and anguish. She cried before the Lord while others misunderstood her. Even the priest Eli thought she was drunk. But God saw her heart. That day, something within her changed. She left the temple without a child, but with a prophetic peace that said, *"It is done."* Soon Samuel, the answer she had prayed for, was placed in her arms.

And then there was **Sarah**, the wife of Abraham, in **Genesis 18 : 9–15**. Her faith had long run dry. She was old, her womb barren, her hope gone. When she overheard the angels telling Abraham, *"Sarah thy wife shall have a son,"* she laughed within herself, saying, *"After I am waxed old shall I have pleasure, my lord being old also?"* But the Lord heard her laugh and asked, *"Is any thing too hard for the Lord?"*

Sometimes we laugh because the promise seems too far-fetched, too late, too impossible. But even our laughter cannot cancel God's word. Sarah conceived and bore

Isaac, and through him came the lineage of promise of *the God of Abraham, Isaac, and Jacob.*

That same God still visits homes that seem forgotten and wombs that seem closed. He specializes in impossible timelines.

Your season of emptiness is not the end, it is the soil where faith takes root. What looks barren is often where God plans to display His glory.

"For all the promises of God in Him are yea, and in Him Amen, unto the glory of God by us." **2 Corinthians 1 : 20 (KJV)**

Sometimes faith must outlast the waiting. It must survive the "not yet." It must believe in the dark what it heard in the light.

Your waiting is not wasted. God does His deepest work in hidden places. When you can't see His hand, trust His heart. When you can't hear His voice, remember His nature. He is good.

Faith that endures emptiness becomes faith that carries abundance with humility.

For Reflection

1. Have you ever mistaken God's silence for His absence?
2. Which woman's story: Sarah, Hannah, or Mary reflects your current season of waiting?

Prophetic Declarations

- My faith is alive even in silence.
- I will believe the Word of the Lord until I see its fulfillment.
- What looks impossible will manifest by the power of God.
- My emptiness is the canvas for God's next miracle.

Prayer

Father, strengthen my faith in the season of silence. Teach me to wait without wavering and to trust without proof. Let my heart believe like Mary, pray like Hannah, and endure like Sarah. Turn my laughter of doubt into laughter of joy. Let Your promises be fulfilled in my life, for they are yes and Amen. In Jesus' mighty name, Amen.

Chapter 7

The Oil of Endurance

Grace to Keep Burning When Others Go Out

"But they that wait upon the LORD shall renew their strength; they shall mount up with wings as eagles; they shall run, and not be weary; and they shall walk, and not faint." **Isaiah 40 : 31 (KJV)**

Endurance is the secret fragrance that Heaven smells in the life of a steadfast woman. It is the perfume of those who keep burning when storms rage, who still worship when others have given up, who stand when the wind tries to bend them.

There are women who can dance in victory, but few who can **wait in warfare** and still keep their flame alive. Endurance is not passive waiting; it is active faith that keeps the lamp trimmed while the Bridegroom tarries.

"While the bridegroom tarried, they all slumbered and slept. And at midnight there was a cry made… Then all those virgins arose, and trimmed their lamps." **Matthew 25 : 5-7 (KJV)**

The parable of the ten virgins teaches that endurance requires **oil,** the inner supply of grace that cannot be borrowed. Five had oil and entered in; five had lamps but no substance. The foolish had light for a moment but no consistency for the night.

Beloved, your lamp is your public life, but your oil is your private devotion. The oil of endurance is produced in secret through tears, prayer, obedience, and worship that no one sees. It is pressed from the olives of your trials.

In seasons when I felt crushed, the Lord whispered, *"Every crushing produces oil."* What you call pressure, Heaven calls preparation. Endurance is proof that you trust God even when you don't understand Him.

Consider **Job**, who sat in ashes, his world reduced to dust, yet he said, *"Though he slay me, yet will I trust in him."* **Job 13 : 15 (KJV)**. That statement still shakes hell today. His endurance became his oil, and his latter end was greater than his beginning.

Think also of **Joseph**, betrayed, imprisoned, and forgotten, yet he kept his integrity. Every delay was a press, every injustice a squeeze that released more fragrance from his spirit. When Pharaoh finally called for him, the oil of endurance had already prepared him for the palace.

And remember **Jesus** in **Gethsemane**, whose very name means "oil press." There, under the weight of destiny, He prayed, *"Nevertheless not my will, but thine, be done."* **Luke 22 : 42 (KJV)**. Out of that pressing flowed redemption for the world.

If you are in a pressing season, do not curse it; collect the oil. It will keep your lamp burning when others' flames go out. The woman who endures becomes a reservoir of power for generations.

"We glory in tribulations also: knowing that tribulation worketh patience; And patience, experience; and experience, hope."
Romans 5 : 3-4 (KJV)

Endurance turns trials into testimonies and pain into perfume. Every moment you refuse to quit, you are being refined into pure oil fit for the King's anointing.

For Reflection

1. In what area of your life is God pressing you to produce oil?
2. How can you keep your inner flame alive while you wait?

Prophetic Declarations

• I will not faint in the day of adversity; my strength is renewed in the Lord.
• My trials are producing oil for my future.
• I am anointed to endure, and my flame will not go out.

Prayer

Father, thank You for the oil that flows from endurance. When I feel pressed, remind me that You are preparing me for purpose. Teach me to wait with worship, to stand with faith, and to shine with perseverance. Let my life carry the fragrance of steadfastness, and may my endurance light the way for others. In Jesus' name, Amen.

Chapter 8

The Woman Who Sees Beyond the Storm

Vision That Outlasts the Wind

"And he arose, and rebuked the wind, and said unto the sea, Peace, be still. And the wind ceased, and there was a great calm." **Mark 4 : 39 (KJV)**

Storms will come. They are not a sign that God has abandoned you; they are often proof that you are carrying something valuable. Every storm in Scripture arose around someone carrying purpose.

The disciples were crossing to the other side when the tempest came. Jesus had said, *"Let us pass over unto the other side."* **Mark 4 : 35 (KJV)**. The storm did not mean they were off course; it meant they were on divine assignment.

Sometimes, the fiercest winds blow when you are closest to breakthrough.

The enemy cannot stop your calling, but he will try to blur your vision with fear. If he can make you panic, he can make you forget what God said. But the woman who sees beyond the storm remembers the promise even when the waves roar.

"For we walk by faith, not by sight." **2 Corinthians 5 : 7 (KJV)**

Faith gives you inner vision when natural sight fails. You can't always control the storm, but you can control your posture in it. The difference between sinking and standing is focus. Peter walked on water until he looked at the waves; the moment his eyes left Jesus, he began to sink.

Beloved, vision keeps you afloat when circumstances try to drown you.

When everything shakes around you - business, family, health - lift your eyes higher. The same voice that said *"Let there be light"* is the same voice that says *"Peace, be still."* Storms do not last forever, but what God plants in you through them will.

Esther: The Woman Who Saw Beyond the Throne

One of the most powerful examples of prophetic vision is **Queen Esther**. Her people faced annihilation under the decree of King Ahasuerus. She knew that approaching the king without being called meant death, yet she also knew that silence would destroy more than her reputation - it would destroy a generation.

"Go, gather together all the Jews that are present in Shushan, and fast ye for me, and neither eat nor drink three days, night or day....so will I go in unto the king, which is not according to the law: and if I perish, I perish." **Esther 4 : 16 (KJV)**

Esther did not rush into the storm; she **prepared** for it. She called for fasting and prayer. She didn't fight with emotion but with intercession. She faced the throne, knowing it could be her last breath, but she looked beyond fear and saw deliverance for her people.

Her courage became her crown. Her obedience opened favor that preserved an entire nation.

Many women today face storms that threaten their homes, children, and future. Some give up too soon because the battle looks bigger than their strength. But Esther's story reminds us: **you were not chosen to run, you were chosen to stand.** There are people, families, and even nations depending on your endurance.

"And who knoweth whether thou art come to the kingdom for such a time as this?" **Esther 4 : 14 (KJV)**

You are not in your position by accident. The very storm surrounding you may be the setup for divine deliverance through you. God placed you in that home, in that ministry, in that city, *for such a time as this.*

When the storm rises, stand like Esther. Fast, pray, and approach your King with boldness. His scepter of favor is already stretched toward you.

Even when the sky is dark, a prophetic woman sees the dawn. She looks at a dead situation and says, *"This too shall pass."* She stands in the gap for her family and says, *"Peace, be still."* She refuses to let her storm dictate her song.

"The LORD shall fight for you, and ye shall hold your peace."

Exodus 14 : 14 (KJV)

When Jesus rebuked the wind, the disciples marveled, saying, *"What manner of man is this, that even the wind and the sea obey him?"* But you, daughter of God, are made in His image. The same authority dwells in you. You can speak peace to the storms within your home, your children, your finances, your ministry.

The storm doesn't define you, it refines you. When the winds settle, you will realize that what you lost was not purpose but fear.

When you see beyond the storm, you start living from the promise, not the pressure.

For Reflection

1. What storm are you currently facing that requires Esther-like courage?
2. How can you prepare spiritually through fasting, prayer, or stillness to face it with vision instead of fear?

Prophetic Declarations

- I will not fear the storm; I carry peace and purpose within me.
- Like Esther, I am positioned for such a time as this.
- I will not perish in the storm; I will rise from it with power.

Prayer

Father, thank You for giving me the eyes to see beyond the storm. Teach me to face life with courage, to fast when I feel faint, and to pray when I feel powerless. Give me the boldness of Esther to rise, to speak, and to save. Let every storm around me bow to Your peace. May my obedience open deliverance for generations after me. In Jesus' name, Amen.

Chapter 9

When the Alabaster Breaks

Worship in the Midst of Pain

"And, behold, a woman in the city, which was a sinner, when she knew that Jesus sat at meat in the Pharisee's house, brought an alabaster box of ointment, And stood at His feet behind Him weeping, and began to wash His feet with tears, and did wipe them with the hairs of her head, and kissed His feet, and anointed them with the ointment." **Luke 7 : 37–38 (KJV)**

There is a worship that only flows from broken places. It is not sung from stages or shouted from crowds, it is whispered through tears when your heart has been crushed, yet still chooses to love God.

The woman with the alabaster box did not come to perform; she came to pour. She brought something precious, something that cost her everything, and she broke it open before Jesus. The fragrance filled the room, and Heaven recognized it.

Pain has a way of producing pure worship. When everything else has failed, what remains is the heart. True worship is not how well you sing but how deeply you surrender.

The alabaster box represents everything you have been saving - your strength, your dignity, your dreams, your hopes. Sometimes God will ask you to break it, not because He wants to destroy you, but because He wants the fragrance to reach places your strength never could.

"The sacrifices of God are a broken spirit: a broken and a contrite heart, O God, thou wilt not despise." **Psalm 51 : 17 (KJV)**

The world despises brokenness, but God dwells in it. Brokenness attracts His presence. The Pharisee who watched that woman judged her, but Jesus defended her. He said, *"She hath wrought a good work upon Me… Verily I say unto you, Wheresoever this gospel shall be preached in the whole world, there shall also this, that this woman hath done, be told for a memorial of her."* **Matthew 26 : 10, 13 (KJV)**

That means your worship in pain is eternal. Heaven remembers your tears. What others call waste, God calls worship.

I have learned that sometimes you must worship through the very thing that tried to destroy you. Worship through betrayal. Worship through disappointment. Worship when you have no words left, because in that soundless cry, Heaven hears your trust.

Like Mary of Bethany, the woman broke what she could not keep and received what she could never lose. That is worship pouring out everything, trusting that what you release into God's hands will never be wasted.

"Though He slay me, yet will I trust in Him." **Job 13 : 15 (KJV)**

Sometimes your alabaster moment is private behind closed doors, when no one understands your pain. Other times it's public, when your praise confuses those who know your story. Either way, your fragrance is noticed in Heaven.

Beloved, when your alabaster breaks, don't gather the pieces - let the oil flow. The same God who saw Mary's tears will see yours.

For Reflection

1. What "alabaster box" have you been holding onto - an area God is asking you to surrender fully?
2. How can your worship become an offering even in the hardest moments?

Prophetic Declarations

- My brokenness is not my end; it is my worship.
- I release everything in me as a fragrance of surrender.
- My pain will produce praise that reaches Heaven.

Prayer

Father, I bring You my alabaster box - every wound, every disappointment, every dream. I break it before You as worship. Let the fragrance of my surrender rise before Your throne. Turn my tears into oil and my sorrow into song. I trust that nothing I give to You is ever wasted. In Jesus' name, Amen.

Chapter 10

The Silent Battles of a Strong Woman

When the Warrior Weeps in Secret

"The LORD is nigh unto them that are of a broken heart; and saveth such as be of a contrite spirit." **Psalm 34 : 18 (KJV)**

There is a pain that has no audience, a war that has no witness, and a strength that is often misunderstood. Many women who appear strong on the outside are quietly fighting battles that no one sees. They carry everyone else's burdens, yet few notice the weight pressing on their own hearts.

Every "strong woman" has a story. Her smile hides scars. Her prayers cover cracks no one else could heal. Yet even in her silence, God hears every unspoken word.

The world expects the strong woman to never bend, never cry, and never rest, but even pillars lean sometimes. It is not weakness to weep; it is worship when tears become prayers.

When I was growing up, we were always told that **a woman never falls sick**. In many African cultures like among the **Kikuyu** of Kenya a woman is seen as the unbreakable pillar of the home. She wakes first and sleeps last. She bears pain silently and is expected to carry the world with a smile.

What baffles me is this: when a child makes a mistake, the community says, *"It is the mother's fault."* But when that same child succeeds or behaves well, they say, *"He has a good father."* The woman's strength is taken for granted, her pain rarely acknowledged.

Even today, in some African communities, a woman is not expected to speak openly about how she feels. She must swallow her tears and keep her dignity. But she is still human. She feels pain, rejection, and betrayal.

As a minister, I have lived this truth. I have loved deeply, embraced people closely, and poured into their lives, yet many turned around and hurt me. Some walked away, only to return later asking for prayer. And still, I prayed for them. I often asked God, *"Why do I keep showing mercy?"*

His answer was gentle: *"Because you carry My heart."*

Even those I opened up to about my pain sometimes repeated the same wound. But I learned not to become numb; I learned to **let go and surrender to God**. The pain a woman carries - especially a woman walking in divine assignment - is indescribable. But in that surrender, I found peace.

Beloved, you who are reading this may be carrying silent battles that no one sees. Maybe you are fighting for your children, your marriage, your ministry, your sanity. You wake up and stand strong while your heart is breaking. You serve while silently bleeding. You smile while fighting spiritual wars no one understands.

But hear this: **you are not a stone; you are chosen.** You feel pain because you carry love. You show mercy because you reflect God. And every tear you have shed is recorded in Heaven.

"When thou passest through the waters, I will be with thee; and through the rivers, they shall not overflow thee." **Isaiah 43 : 2 (KJV)**

Your silence does not mean surrender. Your stillness is not defeat. God is fighting for you even in what you cannot voice.

Even Jesus fought silent battles. In **Luke 22 : 44**, as He prayed in Gethsemane, His sweat was like great drops of blood. No crowd was there, no applause - just pain, surrender, and purpose intertwined. That was the cost of redemption.

So, dear daughter of light, wipe your tears but don't silence your faith. Your tears are intercession. Your sighs are incense. Your private prayers are shaping public testimonies.

Let go and let God take over. When you release it, He restores it. When you stop fighting in your strength, He starts fighting in His.

For Reflection

1. What silent battles have you been carrying that you need to surrender to God today?

2. How can you show yourself the same mercy you show others?

Prophetic Declarations

• My silence is not weakness; it is strength in the presence of God.
• I will let go and let God take over every unseen battle.
• My tears are seeds of restoration and victory.

Prayer

Father, You see what others cannot. You hear the cries I can't put into words. Strengthen me in my silent battles and remind me that Your presence is my refuge. Teach me to let go, to forgive, and to rest in Your grace. I surrender every pain, every disappointment, every betrayal into Your hands. Turn my private struggles into public testimonies of Your mercy. In Jesus' name, Amen.

Chapter 11

When Destiny Demands Separation

The Holy Call to Walk Alone for a While

"And the LORD said unto Abram, Get thee out of thy country, and from thy kindred, and from thy father's house, unto a land that I will shew thee." **Genesis 12 : 1 (KJV)**

There are moments in destiny when God calls you to **come out,** not because people are evil, but because your assignment requires a different atmosphere. Separation is not rejection; it is redirection.

Every woman who carries purpose will walk through seasons where the familiar becomes too small. You begin to feel the stretching of your spirit, the quiet tug of God saying, *"It's time to move."* It's painful when what used to fit no longer feels right, when people you loved suddenly drift away - but in Heaven's calendar, that separation is holy.

Abraham had to leave his father's house before God could make him a father of nations. Moses had to flee Egypt before God could send him back as a deliverer. Jesus withdrew often to pray alone before walking in power before crowds. Solitude is not punishment; it is preparation.

Some women pray for elevation but resist isolation. Yet isolation is the bridge to transformation. When God wants to grow you, He hides you. When He wants to reveal you, He tests you.

"And when he had sent the multitudes away, he went up into a mountain apart to pray." **Matthew 14 : 23 (KJV)**

There will be times you must walk alone, not because people hate you, but because God wants to teach you His voice without distractions. The higher the calling, the smaller the circle.

I remember asking God once, *"Why do people always walk away just when I begin to trust them?"* And He said, *"Because I'm making room for My glory. Some can walk with your pain, but not with your promise."*

Separation exposes motives. It refines your heart. It forces you to depend on God alone. Some people are divine scaffolding. They were there to build you for a season, but not to remain when the building is complete. Don't resent them; release them.

"They went out from us, but they were not of us…" **1 John 2 : 19 (KJV)**

Even **Elijah** had to walk alone before fire fell from Heaven (1 Kings 18). **Esther** had to be separated from her people to be prepared for the palace. **Ruth** had to leave Moab before she could meet Boaz. **Jesus** had to walk the road to Calvary alone before resurrection came.

Sometimes destiny will demand that you travel light without the weight of approval, applause, or company. But hear this, beloved: **when people leave, God stays.**

The absence of some relationships is the presence of divine promotion. Separation is often God's way of moving you into manifestation.

Prophetic Insight: The Seasons of Friendship

In my earlier book, *You Need a Jonathan*, I wrote that friendships are prophetic; they come in **seasons**. Not every friend is meant to last forever; some are assignments, others are lessons, and a few are lifetimes.

Let me take this higher:

Winter Friends

These friends appear when you are in need, when life feels cold and lonely. They come to share warmth, but only for a while. They are like coats useful in the cold, but unnecessary in the heat. Once the storm passes, they fade away.

Summer Friends

These are fair-weather companions. They shine bright when everything in your life is glowing. They celebrate your victories but disappear at the first sign of clouds. They love the light but cannot handle the shadows.

Fall Friends

These ones walk away just when you need them most. Like leaves, they detach at the first strong wind and never return. But even they have purpose; they teach you who cannot go with you into the next season.

Spring Friends

These are divine connectors sent by God. They appear suddenly, bringing refreshment and restoration. They don't come to take; they come to *add*. Sometimes you never knew them before, but they show up at the right time to speak life, to support, to build. These are covenant friendships; God-sent like **Jonathan to David**.

"And Jonathan stripped himself of the robe that was upon him, and gave it to David, and his garments, even to his sword, and to his bow, and to his girdle." **1 Samuel 18 : 4 (KJV)**

Jonathan wasn't just a friend; he was a bridge between David's anointing and his throne. Every destiny needs a Jonathan - someone who covers you in your waiting season and celebrates you when you rise.

But remember, not everyone is a Jonathan. Some are Sauls, intimidated by your calling. Others are Ahithophels, offended by your truth. That's why God allows separation to sift your circle and preserve your peace.

So, when people walk away, bless them and release them. Don't chase what God has chosen to remove. What is meant for your next season will meet you there.

For Reflection

1. Which friendships in your life are seasonal, and which ones are covenantal?
2. How can you discern when a relationship's season has ended without bitterness?

Prophetic Declarations

• I will no longer mourn expired seasons; I celebrate divine timing.
• God is aligning me with covenant relationships for destiny.
• I bless those who left, and I embrace those God sends.

Prayer

Father, thank You for every person You brought into my life for a reason or a season. Give me the wisdom to discern the difference between temporary and eternal connections. Remove what distracts me, and position those who will walk with me into destiny. Help me to love without clinging, to release without resentment, and to embrace divine separation as sacred preparation. In Jesus' mighty name, Amen.

Chapter 12

The Power of Forgiveness

Releasing Yourself to Rise Again

"And be ye kind one to another, tenderhearted, forgiving one another, even as God for Christ's sake hath forgiven you."
Ephesians 4 : 32 (KJV)

Forgiveness is one of the hardest lessons on the road to healing. It is easy to preach about forgiveness until you are the one holding the pain. Yet forgiveness is the doorway to freedom - the place where your spirit begins to breathe again.

Unforgiveness is like drinking poison and expecting another to die. It doesn't punish your offender; it imprisons your purpose. Forgiveness doesn't make what happened right, it simply releases you from being chained to it.

There was a season when I struggled to forgive myself. I kept asking God, *"How did I let this happen? Why did I trust them? Why did I give so much?"* I had poured out everything: time, ideas, prayers, and love, only to be betrayed and misunderstood. I wasn't just angry with other people; I was angry with myself.

But then, in His mercy, the Lord whispered, *"Daughter, even that pain has purpose. I allowed it to grow you."*

I realized that forgiveness begins with self. If you cannot forgive yourself, you will never truly heal.

The Aroma of Forgiveness: Stories from Scripture

"But while he was yet a great way off, his father saw him, and had compassion, and ran, and fell on his neck, and kissed him." **Luke 15 : 20 (KJV)**

The **Prodigal Son** walked away from his father, wasted his inheritance, and returned home expecting rejection. Instead, he met mercy. His father ran toward him, not with anger, but with open arms. That's how Heaven responds when repentance meets forgiveness.

True forgiveness smells like grace; it carries a fragrance that attracts favor from both **God and men**. When you forgive, your life begins to release an aroma that pleases Heaven.

"Then Peter remembered the word of Jesus… and he went out, and wept bitterly." **Matthew 26 : 75 (KJV)**

Peter denied Jesus three times, yet after his tears came restoration. Jesus didn't disqualify him, He recommissioned him: *"Feed My sheep."* (John 21 : 17). Forgiveness turned Peter from a man of failure into a pillar of faith.

But **Judas Iscariot**, who also betrayed Jesus, failed to forgive himself. Instead of running back to grace, he ran toward guilt. His despair led to destruction.

The difference between Peter and Judas wasn't the size of their sin, it was the state of their hearts. One sought mercy; the other surrendered to shame.

Forgiveness of others and forgiveness of self are like two wings of the same dove; you cannot fly in peace without both.

When you release others, you open the heavens over your life. When you release yourself, you open your destiny.

"Joseph said unto them, Fear not: for am I in the place of God? … ye thought evil against me; but God meant it unto good." **Genesis 50 : 19–20 (KJV)**

Joseph's forgiveness restored his family; the father's forgiveness restored the prodigal; Jesus' forgiveness restored the world. Forgiveness is not weakness, it is divine strength disguised as surrender.

For Reflection

1. Are you carrying guilt that God has already forgiven?
2. Whom must you forgive so that the fragrance of favor can rest upon you again?

Prophetic Declarations

- Forgiveness flows from me like a heavenly aroma.
- I forgive others and myself, and I walk in divine favor.

- My mercy invites Heaven's mercy; my release attracts restoration.

Prayer

Father, thank You for showing me that forgiveness is freedom.
Teach me to forgive others as You forgave me, and to forgive myself where I have fallen short. Let my heart release a fragrance that draws Your favor and peace. May I, like the prodigal, find arms of compassion, like Peter, rise again in purpose, and never, like Judas, surrender to despair. In Jesus' mighty name, Amen.

Chapter 13

Love That Learns: When Betrayal Becomes a Teacher

Healing the Heart Without Losing Its Power

"But I say unto you, Love your enemies, bless them that curse you, do good to them that hate you, and pray for them which despitefully use you, and persecute you." **Matthew 5 : 44 (KJV)**

Betrayal is one of the most painful experiences a person can endure. It feels like a knife from behind, coming from hands that once held yours. Yet if you allow God to interpret your pain, you will see that **betrayal was never meant to break you, it was meant to build you.**

Every betrayal carries a hidden promotion. What you thought was rejection was actually redirection. What you saw as loss was really God removing the wrong foundation so that your destiny could stand on the right one.

There was a time in my life when betrayal cut so deep that I questioned love itself. I had poured my soul into people, mentored them, blessed them, prayed for them, shared ideas and visions, only to see them walk away without gratitude. Some even turned against me. I wept before God and asked, *"Why does love always hurt the giver?"*

The Spirit of the Lord whispered, *"Because true love must first be tested before it can be trusted."*

That was when I understood: **betrayal doesn't come to destroy you; it comes to reveal you.**

When Love Meets the Test of Betrayal

In **2 Samuel 15 - 18**, King **David** faced the betrayal of his own son, **Absalom**. The pain of that moment was greater than any battle he had fought. The one he raised turned to ruin him. But when Absalom died, David didn't celebrate, he mourned:

"O my son Absalom, my son, my son Absalom! would God I had died for thee." **2 Samuel 18 : 33 (KJV)**

That's love purified through pain. Betrayal revealed the depth of David's heart. It didn't harden him; it humbled him.

Your reaction to betrayal determines your resurrection. If you respond with bitterness, you block your blessing; but if you respond with brokenness before God, He builds you back stronger.

Samson and Delilah

When Desire Blinds Discernment

"And she made him sleep upon her knees; and she called for a man, and she caused him to shave off the seven locks of his head…"
Judges 16 : 19 (KJV)

Samson was anointed from birth, chosen to deliver Israel, yet he fell into the trap of misplaced affection. **Delilah** didn't love Samson; she loved his secret. Her betrayal exposed the danger of giving your heart to those who can't guard your anointing.

But even after his failure, Samson's story didn't end in shame. In **Judges 16 : 22**, the Scripture says:

"Howbeit the hair of his head began to grow again after he was shaven."

That verse still carries resurrection power. It means your strength can return after betrayal. What you lost in weakness can be restored in worship. God never ends your story with your mistake; He ends it with mercy.

Betrayal Should Build You, Not Break You

When betrayal comes, it's easy to get angry, bitter, and defensive. But remember: **those who betray you often unlock what was hidden inside you.**

Joseph's brothers sold him into slavery, but it was that betrayal that positioned him for the palace. Had they not rejected him, he would never have met Pharaoh. What they meant for evil, God turned for good.

"But as for you, ye thought evil against me; but God meant it unto good." **Genesis 50 : 20 (KJV)**

So many people hate those who betrayed them, not realizing those very betrayals were midwives to their destiny. The cross was not just the place of Jesus' suffering, it was also the stage of His glory. The betrayal of Judas did not end Jesus' ministry; it fulfilled His mission.

If Jesus had to be betrayed to reach resurrection, what makes us think we can rise without pain?

"If we suffer, we shall also reign with him." **2 Timothy 2 : 12 (KJV)**

Every betrayal is a classroom. It teaches you discernment, boundaries, and divine dependence. It shows you who was with you for the miracles and who could walk with you through the midnight.

Betrayal reveals the purity of your love. It tests whether you loved people for who they were, or for what they could do for you.

Love That Learns

Love that learns does not stop loving. It simply loves wisely. It discerns without despising. It blesses without bonding. It gives, but guards.

When you learn through betrayal, you come out with sharper discernment and deeper compassion. You learn to trust the Spirit more than faces, to listen to peace more than promises.

Even Jesus, knowing Judas would betray Him, still washed his feet (John 13 : 5 - 11). That's love matured through revelation. It serves without seeking validation.

"Charity suffereth long, and is kind… beareth all things, believeth all things, hopeth all things, endureth all things." **1 Corinthians 13 : 4,7 (KJV)**

Betrayal cannot destroy a heart that's anchored in God's love - it only strengthens its roots.

For Reflection

1. What has betrayal taught you about love and discernment?
2. Are you allowing your betrayal to build you or break you?

Prophetic Declarations

- Betrayal will build me, not break me.
- I am wiser, stronger, and more discerning because of what I've endured.
- I will love without losing my guard and forgive without losing my boundaries.

Prayer

Father, thank You for turning betrayal into a bridge to my breakthrough. Heal the wounds that came from those I trusted, and teach me to see the divine lesson in every disappointment. I refuse to let pain harden my heart. I choose to be refined, not ruined, strengthened, not shattered. Let Your love rebuild me into the woman You created me to be: whole, wise, and walking in grace. In Jesus' mighty name, Amen.

Chapter 14

The Rise of the Deborah Generation

When Women Stand, Nations Shift

"And Deborah, a prophetess, the wife of Lapidoth, she judged Israel at that time." **Judges 4 : 4 (KJV)**

There comes a moment in history when Heaven looks for a voice - not just a preacher, but a prophetess; not just a mother, but a midwife of destiny. We are living in that moment now. The world is crying for the manifestation of the daughters of God - women who will rise in holiness, courage, and obedience to divine purpose.

This is the hour of **The Deborah Generation** - a generation of women who lead with purity, war with prayer, build with wisdom, and love with power. These are women who have been through pain but refuse to stay there; they rise not for recognition, but for restoration.

Deborah: The Mother of Nations

When Israel was in bondage, when men hid in fear and the nation had lost direction, God raised a woman, **Deborah**. She was not trained as a warrior nor crowned as a queen, yet Heaven trusted her voice to lead a people back to victory.

"I, Deborah, arose… a mother in Israel." **Judges 5 : 7 (KJV)**

Deborah's authority came from her submission to God. She didn't rise in pride; she rose in purpose. She didn't compete with men; she completed God's assignment. When she summoned **Barak**, she didn't shame him for fear; she strengthened him through prophecy.

That is the true anointing of a Deborah: **to awaken courage in others through faith in God.**

Ruth: The Power of Obedience and Humility

Alongside Deborah's boldness stands another woman of great virtue **Ruth.** Ruth's strength was not seen in battle but in **obedience, loyalty, and submission.**

After losing her husband, Ruth could have chosen comfort, but instead, she chose covenant. She told Naomi,

"Whither thou goest, I will go; and where thou lodgest, I will lodge: thy people shall be my people, and thy God my God." **Ruth 1 : 16 (KJV)**

Ruth didn't chase position; she pursued purpose. She followed Naomi with humility, listened to her counsel, and obeyed divine instruction.

When Naomi told her how to approach **Boaz**, she didn't argue; she submitted. That obedience positioned her for divine favor.

"And he said, Blessed be thou of the LORD, my daughter: for thou hast shewed more kindness in the latter end than at the beginning."
Ruth 3 : 10 (KJV)

Ruth's humility opened the door that pride could never unlock.
Her name became written into the lineage of kings - the genealogy of **Jesus Christ** (Matthew 1 : 5).

A true Deborah is not loud in self-promotion; she is loud in obedience. She doesn't boast in what she can do but in what God can do through her.

A true Deborah carries the boldness of a lion and the humility of a lamb. She knows that authority without humility becomes arrogance, and gifting without submission becomes rebellion.

The Call of the Deborah Generation

The Deborah Generation is not made of women who seek titles, but women who seek transformation. They carry the womb of intercession and the mantle of leadership. They are warriors and nurturers, prophets and mothers, builders and intercessors - moving in harmony with Heaven's rhythm.

"For such a time as this..." **Esther 4 : 14 (KJV)**

Like **Esther**, they fast, pray, and take risks for their people.

Like **Deborah**, they decree and lead. Like **Ruth**, they submit, serve, and obey, even in pain.

And like **Mary**, they say, *"Be it unto me according to thy word."* **Luke 1 : 38 (KJV)**

This is the divine balance: boldness and brokenness, leadership and submission, strength and surrender.

A True Deborah Never Stops Moving Forward

A true Deborah doesn't allow pain to paralyze her. Even when betrayed, misunderstood, or overlooked, she keeps pressing forward. She knows her strength doesn't come from applause but from assignment.

"Forgetting those things which are behind, and reaching forth unto those things which are before." **Philippians 3 : 13 (KJV)**

Pain becomes her teacher, not her prison. Disappointment becomes her classroom, not her coffin.

Deborahs don't quit; they **rise again and again**. They are resilient because they have died to pride and come alive to purpose. They stand firm because they are anchored in obedience.

The Characteristics of the Deborah Generation

1. **They Hear God Clearly.**
   They tune out noise and tune in to Heaven. They walk in discernment, not emotion.
2. **They War Through Worship.**

They lift praise in pain and shift atmospheres with prayer.
3. **They Build in the Midst of Chaos.**
When others give up, they rise to rebuild.
4. **They Carry Motherhood in Spirit.**
Whether naturally or spiritually, they birth others into destiny.
5. **They Are Humble, Yet Powerful.**
6. Like Ruth, they move in quiet strength - trusting obedience over pride.

For Reflection

1. What area of your life is God calling you to rise in obedience and humility?
2. Are you walking with the courage of Deborah and the submission of Ruth?

Prophetic Declarations

• I am part of the Deborah Generation: bold yet humble, strong yet surrendered.
• I carry the obedience of Ruth and the authority of Deborah.
• My pain will never stop my purpose, and my humility will attract Heaven's favor.

Prayer

Father, thank You for raising women of purpose in this generation. Clothe me with the mantle of Deborah and the spirit of Ruth. Teach me to walk in power without pride, and in strength without striving. May obedience open doors that talent cannot. I rise in Your authority to lead, serve, and love with grace. In Jesus' mighty name, Amen.

Chapter 15

The Power of a Prophetic Woman's Voice

When She Speaks, the Heavens Listen

"Death and life are in the power of the tongue: and they that love it shall eat the fruit thereof." **Proverbs 18 : 21 (KJV)**

A woman's voice carries power - creative, destructive, transformative power. When a woman speaks under the leading of the Holy Spirit, her words become weapons and her declarations shift nations.

Heaven has always used women to speak into destiny. In Genesis, God's first recorded conversation with a woman was with **Eve**. Though deception entered through words, redemption also began through a woman's declaration: **Mary's "Be it unto me according to thy word."**

"And Mary said, Behold the handmaid of the Lord; be it unto me according to thy word." **Luke 1 : 38 (KJV)**

Mary's agreement with Heaven birthed the Savior. Her voice released life into existence. Every woman reading this must understand: **your words are wombs** - they conceive realities.

Your Tongue Is a Gate of Creation

God's first act in Genesis was to **speak.** Ten times He said, *"Let there be…"* and the universe responded. (Genesis 1) A prophetic woman carries that same divine DNA. When she opens her mouth in faith, the earth must align with Heaven's decree.

Your voice is not ordinary; it is divine breath wrapped in flesh. When you speak life, Heaven echoes. When you speak doubt, darkness gains ground.

"Thou shalt also decree a thing, and it shall be established unto thee: and the light shall shine upon thy ways." **Job 22 : 28 (KJV)**

Every prophetic woman must guard her speech. You cannot carry both blessing and bitterness in the same mouth. Your words either build your future or bury it. Speak as a builder, not as a breaker.

Deborah's Voice of Judgment and Victory

When **Deborah** spoke, her words carried divine authority. She didn't lift a sword; she lifted a decree.

"Up; for this is the day in which the LORD hath delivered Sisera into thine hand." **Judges 4 : 14 (KJV)**

Her voice ignited courage in Barak and caused a fearful army to rise. Prophetic women do not need to shout to be powerful. Their power flows through obedience and clarity of utterance. When Deborah spoke, nations shifted.

A true prophetic voice does not speak opinions; it speaks revelation. A Deborah does not echo emotion; she declares instruction.

Hannah: The Voice That Births a Prophet

Hannah was mocked by Peninnah and misunderstood by Eli, yet she turned her pain into prophecy. Her tears became her language. Her groaning became intercession. When she spoke from her spirit, Heaven responded with **Samuel,** a prophet who anointed kings.

"For this child I prayed; and the LORD hath given me my petition which I asked of him." **1 Samuel 1 : 27 (KJV)**

Hannah teaches us that not every prayer needs words, but every word must carry prayer. Your pain is not wasted when it becomes your message.

Esther: The Voice That Saved a Nation

Esther understood timing and tone. She didn't rush into the king's presence with emotion; she prepared through fasting and prayer. When she finally spoke, her words carried the weight of Heaven's wisdom.

"If I perish, I perish." **Esther 4 : 16 (KJV)**

Her intercession saved generations. That's the power of a woman who knows when and how to speak.

Beloved, silence can be holy, but when God tells you to speak, your voice becomes the sound of deliverance.

The Prophetic Voice in You

Every woman has a prophetic sound. Some speak through preaching, others through prayer, writing, leadership, business, or motherhood. Whatever your platform, your voice is needed.

There are nations waiting for your decree, children waiting for your blessing, cities waiting for your intercession, and families waiting for your song.

Do not silence yourself because of pain or people's opinions. Your voice is not a mistake; it is a mandate.

"Cry aloud, spare not, lift up thy voice like a trumpet." **Isaiah 58 : 1 (KJV)**

Every word you speak in faith becomes a trumpet in the Spirit, awakening what has been dormant.

The Deborah Generation does not complain; they **command.** They don't gossip; they **prophesy.** They don't react; they **release decrees.**

Guarding Your Voice

Your voice carries destiny, but it can also be polluted. Guard your heart so your mouth stays pure. Don't allow bitterness to become your language or anger to become your anthem.

"Set a watch, O LORD, before my mouth; keep the door of my lips." **Psalm 141 : 3 (KJV)**

You cannot release healing if your heart is still bleeding. Before you speak over others, let God speak over you. Let your words carry grace, wisdom, and truth seasoned with love and saturated with power.

For Reflection

1. Have you been silencing your voice out of fear or past pain?
2. What prophetic words has God placed in your spirit that you must now declare?

Prophetic Declarations

- My voice carries the sound of Heaven.
- I decree life, favor, and restoration over every dry place.
- My words are weapons of creation, not destruction.
- I will no longer be silent; I will speak and nations will respond.

Prayer

Father, thank You for the gift of my voice. Anoint my words with power and purity. Let my declarations carry Heaven's authority and manifest Your will on earth. Silence every voice of fear that tries to quiet mine. Use me as Your trumpet to decree life, healing, and revival in my generation. In Jesus' mighty name, Amen.

Chapter 16

The Woman and the Seed

The Womb That Carries Nations

"And I will put enmity between thee and the woman, and between thy seed and her seed; it shall bruise thy head, and thou shalt bruise his heel." **Genesis 3 : 15 (KJV)**

From the beginning of creation, the greatest battle ever fought has been over *the seed*. The enemy fears the womb of a woman because it is the gateway through which Heaven introduces change. Every revival, every deliverance, every move of God begins with a woman who dares to carry something divine.

You are not just a woman; you are a **divine vessel**, a carrier of prophecy. You are a **walking covenant**, holding within you the potential to birth what eyes have not seen and ears have not heard.

Every woman carries a seed: a dream, an idea, a destiny hidden within her by God.

The enemy doesn't attack a woman because of who she is; he attacks her because of what she carries. He knows that inside her lies the next Samuel, the next Esther, the next Deborah, the next movement of God.

The Seed Carries a Star

"And, lo, the star, which they saw in the east, went before them, till it came and stood over where the young child was." **Matthew 2 : 9 (KJV)**

When Jesus was born, His star appeared in the heavens. Every divine seed carries its own light - its own signature in the spirit realm. That is why your life shines differently when you carry divine purpose.

The womb of a woman is not just biological, it is spiritual. It is a place of creation, incubation, and manifestation. When you conceive a vision, a purpose, or an assignment from God, that seed already glows with heavenly identity.

Every woman carries a *star* waiting for manifestation. Guard it, nurture it, and speak over it, because Heaven has already said, *"Let there be light."*

Hannah: The Womb of Intercession

Hannah cried out to God, not because she wanted to prove her worth, but because she knew her barrenness had a purpose. Her seed, **Samuel**, was not just a child, he was the answer to a nation's silence.

"For this child I prayed; and the LORD hath given me my petition which I asked of him." **1 Samuel 1 : 27 (KJV)**

When a woman's prayer aligns with Heaven's purpose, barrenness becomes a birthing ground. Your tears are not wasted, they are the water that nourishes your seed.

Elizabeth: The Womb of Revival

"And, behold, thy cousin Elisabeth, she hath also conceived a son in her old age: and this is the sixth month with her, who was called barren." **Luke 1 : 36 (KJV)**

Elizabeth, the mother of **John the Baptist**, represents divine timing. She carried a prophetic seed that would *prepare the way of the Lord*. Even when her body was considered too old, Heaven declared, *"It is not over."*

The delay was not denial, it was divine scheduling. Her womb was reserved for a voice that would awaken generations.

Sometimes your promise doesn't come early because it must arrive at a time when it can influence others divinely connected to your destiny, like how John's birth aligned with Jesus'.

When God finally visits your "barren" season, He does it in such a way that everyone who doubted will know *"The Lord hath done great things."* (**Luke 1 : 58 KJV**)

Rebekah: The Womb of Covenant

"And the LORD said unto her, Two nations are in thy womb, and two manner of people shall be separated from thy bowels." **Genesis 25 : 23 (KJV)**

Rebekah, the wife of Isaac and mother of **Jacob and Esau**, carried nations inside her. Even before their birth,

God spoke destiny over her womb. She wasn't just carrying children, she was carrying *prophecy*.

When she felt turmoil within, she sought God directly: *"If it be so, why am I thus* (**Genesis 25 : 22 KJV**)*?"* And the Lord revealed that her womb held a battle of generations.

Sometimes the conflict you feel within is not confusion, it's destiny wrestling to emerge. The pain in your spirit is the sign of purpose pressing for birth.

Rebekah reminds us that some wombs carry not one purpose but two: two nations, two generations, two movements, and discernment is needed to guide them rightly.

Mary: The Womb That Carried the Word

"The Holy Ghost shall come upon thee, and the power of the Highest shall overshadow thee." **Luke 1 : 35 (KJV)**

When **Mary** said *"Be it unto me according to thy word,"* she opened the gate for redemption. Her submission turned divine prophecy into divine pregnancy.

You too carry promises that require your "yes." Every "yes" births something that changes history.

You may not birth the Messiah, but you may birth a ministry, a movement, a solution, or a generational change.

The Holy Spirit is still overshadowing daughters who believe.

Ruth: The Womb of Legacy

"And Boaz took Ruth… and she bare a son… and they called his name Obed: he is the father of Jesse, the father of David." **Ruth 4 : 13, 17 (KJV)**

Ruth's obedience positioned her for divine connection. Her submission to Naomi's counsel became the bridge to the lineage of Christ.

Ruth didn't chase fame, she followed faith. Her humility birthed a legacy. Every time you obey God's instruction, you secure your spiritual genealogy.

Your womb, spiritual and physical, is a generational key. What you carry can rewrite history.

Guard the Seed You Carry

Every attack against you is proof of what you carry. Pharaoh sought to kill Moses; Herod sought to kill Jesus. The greater the attack, the greater the assignment.

"He that goeth forth and weepeth, bearing precious seed, shall doubtless come again with rejoicing." **Psalm 126 : 6 (KJV)**

Guard your seed through prayer, purity, and perseverance. Speak life over it. Protect it from negativity. Water it with worship until it breaks the ground.

Even if your season looks quiet, know that the seed is working in silence.

For Reflection

1. What has God deposited inside you that you've forgotten or stopped nurturing?
2. Are you guarding your seed like Rebekah, nurturing it like Hannah, and believing like Elizabeth?

Prophetic Declarations

- I am a carrier of divine prophecy and purpose.
- My womb is a sanctuary for Heaven's will.
- Every seed I carry will live, grow, and shine.
- The delay in my promise is not denial; it's divine timing.

Prayer

Father, thank You for entrusting me with divine seed. I declare that every promise You've placed within me will manifest in Your perfect time. Like Hannah, I will pray; like Elizabeth, I will believe; like Rebekah, I will inquire; and like Mary, I will surrender. Overshadow me, Lord, and bring forth what You have planted in me. In Jesus' mighty name, Amen.

Chapter 17

When Pain Becomes a Platform

Your Brokenness Is the Bridge to Someone Else's Breakthrough

"And we know that all things work together for good to them that love God, to them who are the called according to his purpose." **Romans 8 : 28 (KJV)**

Pain is not the end of your story; it is the beginning of your platform. Every tear, every heartbreak, every betrayal, and every loss was not destruction - it was construction. God was not breaking you to bury you; He was breaking you to build you.

When life shattered around you, Heaven was secretly rearranging your foundation. He does His greatest work in hidden places where no applause is heard, and no spotlight shines.

Beloved, your pain is not wasted. It is a *divine investment* in your purpose.

Joseph: The Platform of the Pit

Joseph's brothers stripped him of his coat but could not strip him of his calling. What looked like rejection was actually redirection.

"But as for you, ye thought evil against me; but God meant it unto good." **Genesis 50 : 20 (KJV)**

Every pit has a purpose. Every betrayal has a blueprint. The same brothers who betrayed him were the ones who bowed before him. The same prison that confined him was the passageway to Pharaoh's palace.

You may be in a pit now - overlooked, forgotten, or misunderstood, but God is using that place to prepare your platform.

When He finally elevates you, you will look back and realize: *"If I hadn't been broken, I wouldn't have been built."*

Naomi: The Platform of the Bitter Season

Naomi lost her husband and sons and renamed herself **Mara**, meaning *bitter*. Yet even in her bitterness, God was aligning her destiny with **Ruth**, who would restore joy and lineage.

"Call me not Naomi, call me Mara: for the Almighty hath dealt very bitterly with me." **Ruth 1 : 20 (KJV)**

Sometimes your pain will attract people who are part of your redemption. Ruth didn't come to Naomi in her laughter; she came in her loss.

Pain will often reveal your Ruth - the one assigned to walk you into your next season. Through Naomi's pain came Ruth's purpose, and through Ruth's obedience came Jesus' lineage.

Your bitter season can birth another woman's breakthrough.

Job: The Platform of Restoration

Job lost everything - children, wealth, and health, yet he never cursed God. Even when misunderstood by friends, he chose worship over wrath.

"Though he slay me, yet will I trust in him." **Job 13 : 15 (KJV)**

When the test was over, God restored **double** what he lost. Sometimes God allows the shaking to prove the stability of your foundation.

Job's story teaches us that pain refines, not defines. Your endurance becomes your elevation.

Daniel and the Three Hebrew Boys: The Platform of the Fire

Not all pain comes from betrayal. Some comes from standing for truth.

Shadrach, Meshach, and Abednego refused to bow before the king's image. Their conviction cost them comfort; their faith led them straight into the fire. But what man meant to consume them, God used to *reveal Himself through them.*

"Our God whom we serve is able to deliver us… but if not, be it known unto thee, O king, that we will not serve thy gods." **Daniel 3 : 17–18 (KJV)**

That is faith refined in fire - a faith that stands whether or not God performs.

When the king looked into the furnace, he saw a fourth man, *the Son of God,* walking with them. Your fiery trial is often where Jesus appears most clearly.

The same fire that should have burned them only burned their chains. Your trial is not meant to destroy you, but to deliver you from what once bound you.

"The fire had no power, nor was an hair of their head singed." **Daniel 3 : 27 (KJV)**

When God brings you out, you won't even smell like what you've been through. The very furnace that exposed you will become your elevation.

"Then the king promoted Shadrach, Meshach, and Abednego, in the province of Babylon." **Daniel 3 : 30 (KJV)**

Their pain promoted them; their stand made them seen.

And when **Daniel** himself was cast into the lions' den, he prayed as usual and trusted God.

"My God hath sent his angel, and hath shut the lions' mouths." **Daniel 6 : 22 (KJV)**

God didn't keep him from the den; He kept him *in* it. Sometimes the miracle is not in avoidance, but in protection during the storm.

The lions were real, but the peace of God was greater. The den became Daniel's pulpit; his pain became his platform.

Jesus: The Platform of the Cross

No greater example exists than Jesus Himself. He was betrayed, denied, mocked, wounded, and crucified. Yet it was *that pain* that became *the platform* for humanity's redemption.

"Who for the joy that was set before him endured the cross, despising the shame." **Hebrews 12 : 2 (KJV)**

The cross was not a tragedy; it was a transaction. His wounds became our healing; His pain became our platform for grace.

When you walk with God, nothing is wasted - not even your scars. What the world sees as shame, Heaven calls strategy.

Prophetic Insight: Pain Is a Seed

Pain is a seed that births power when planted in God's presence. Every disappointment has divine DNA. It carries the potential to multiply once surrendered to God.

"They that sow in tears shall reap in joy." **Psalm 126 : 5 (KJV)**

When you stop running from pain and start learning from it, it becomes your greatest teacher. Your testimony will speak louder than your trauma.

Pain refines your compassion. It gives you eyes to see the hurting, ears to hear the broken, and a voice that carries healing.

"For our light affliction, which is but for a moment, worketh for us a far more exceeding and eternal weight of glory." **2 Corinthians 4 : 17 (KJV)**

Every weight of pain produces the weight of glory.

Your Story Is the Oil Someone Else Needs

When you've walked through the fire and come out refined, your story becomes someone else's survival guide. That's why God didn't let it kill you, because He needed your voice on the other side.

A woman who has conquered pain carries a fragrance that Heaven recognizes - the aroma of crushed oil.

The anointing is never cheap. It comes from being pressed, squeezed, and crushed just like olives that produce oil.

"Out of the eater came forth meat, and out of the strong came forth sweetness." **Judges 14 : 14 (KJV)**

Samson's riddle reminds us: What once devoured you can now feed you.

For Reflection

1. What "fire" or "den" have you walked through that revealed God's presence in new ways?
2. How can your scars become someone else's signpost of hope?

Prophetic Declarations

• My pain is becoming my platform.
• My scars are turning into songs of victory.
• Every tear I've shed will produce a harvest of healing.
• What tried to break me will bless me.
• I will come out of the fire without the smell of smoke.

Prayer

Father, thank You for turning my pain into purpose. Every experience that once wounded me is now working for my good. Use my story to heal others, my scars to testify, and my voice to lift those still in darkness. Transform every tear into triumph and every valley into victory. Let my life be proof that pain births power when placed in Your hands. In Jesus' mighty name, Amen.

Prophetic Summary

This chapter completes the revelation that pain is never punishment; it's preparation. From **Joseph's pit, Naomi's loss, Job's endurance, Daniel's lions,** and the **fire of the Hebrew boys,** all the way to **the Cross,** each story proves: *Pain is Heaven's platform where faith becomes visible and glory becomes public.*

Chapter 18

You Are a Nation

Awakening the Seed of Nations Within You

"And the LORD said unto her, Two nations are in thy womb, and two manner of people shall be separated from thy bowels." **Genesis 25 : 23 (KJV)**

When God looks at a woman, He doesn't see one person; He sees a nation. You are not just a voice; you are a generation waiting to rise. Every time you speak, a nation shifts; every time you pray, a generation is preserved.

Heaven never designed you to be small. Your spirit is territorial; your purpose is continental. You carry within you the capacity to birth, build, and bless.

When God Calls a Woman, He Raises a Generation

"Before I formed thee in the belly I knew thee." **Jeremiah 1 : 5 (KJV)**

When God called **Deborah**, He wasn't raising one judge. He was raising a deliverance for a whole nation. When He called **Mary**, He wasn't just calling a teenager in Nazareth. He was birthing redemption for the world. When He called **Esther**, He wasn't simply saving a people. He was shifting a kingdom.

Every woman who answers the call of God becomes a voice for nations, even if her feet never leave her home.

You Are a Prophetic Gate

In the spirit realm, a woman is a gate - the door through which destinies enter the earth.

When you open your mouth to declare God's word, you legislate change in the atmosphere. Your words become keys that unlock families, cities, and nations.

That is why the enemy fights a woman's voice. He knows that a woman who understands her authority in God cannot be silenced.

"Cry aloud, thou that didst not travail with child: for more are the children of the desolate than the children of the married wife, saith the LORD." **Isaiah 54 : 1 (KJV)**

Your cries in prayer carry the sound of birth. Your intercession gives life to movements you may never see with your eyes.

From Wilderness to Nationhood

"And the LORD found him in a desert land… He kept him as the apple of His eye." **Deuteronomy 32 : 10 (KJV)**

Nations are not born in comfort; they are forged in wilderness seasons. The time you felt abandoned was when God was forming your identity.

Your pain was not a punishment; it was a passport. He was training you to handle nations. Every storm you survived was spiritual boot camp for kingdom assignment.

When you rise, others rise with you. When you heal, entire bloodlines heal.

You Carry the Blueprint of Nations

Sarah laughed when God promised her a child, yet from her womb came a nation called Israel. **Rebekah** carried two nations inside her womb - Jacob and Esau. **Mary** carried a King who would reign over all nations.

You too carry a blueprint. Maybe it's a business, a ministry, a movement, or a voice that will heal a generation. Whatever it is, it is bigger than you.

Don't downsize your calling to fit the expectations of those who don't see what God showed you.

Prophetic Picture: A Woman as a Nation

When a woman prays, Heaven listens like a nation is speaking. When she cries, Heaven moves like a government in session. When she rises, darkness shifts its boundaries.

You are not a name on paper. You are a living altar of purpose.

Inside you flows the economy of grace, the currency of faith, and the constitution of the Kingdom.

"Ye are a chosen generation, a royal priesthood, an holy nation." **1 Peter 2 : 9 (KJV)**

Heaven calls you a holy nation because you carry the DNA of divine government.

Don't Let Pain Make You Silent

Many women lose their voice after betrayal or disappointment, but this is the hour to speak again. A silent woman cannot govern a nation.

In all my years of ministry, I've noticed that many women think about solutions, envision change, or imagine breakthroughs but they never *speak* them out. They keep the vision locked inside their minds and expect transformation, yet Heaven responds not to thought but to *sound*.

Thinking is different from declaring. The mind conceives, but the mouth creates.

When God created the world, He didn't meditate the universe into existence; He *spoke* it.

"And God said, Let there be light: and there was light." **Genesis 1 : 3 (KJV)**

The atmosphere does not obey thoughts; it obeys decrees. As a prophetess, when I move in the Spirit, I do not stay silent; I *declare*. Every time I open my mouth to prophesy, I am commanding the unseen to manifest the will of Heaven.

Women of God, this is your time to rise and speak. Your voice carries legislative authority. When you decree healing, Heaven releases it. When you prophesy life, the dry bones begin to move.

"Prophesy upon these bones, and say unto them, O ye dry bones, hear the word of the LORD." **Ezekiel 37 : 4 (KJV)**

Thinking may inspire you, but speaking will *activate* you. Your declaration is the bridge between the promise and the manifestation.

"Death and life are in the power of the tongue." **Proverbs 18 : 21 (KJV)**

A woman who understands this truth never lets pain silence her again. She doesn't just think change - she **declares** it. She doesn't just dream; she **decrees**. Because she knows that her mouth is the womb of miracles.

For Reflection

1. What nations are hidden within your purpose that you've not yet spoken to life?
2. Where have you allowed fear or pain to silence your prophetic voice?

Prophetic Declarations

- I am not just a woman; I am a nation.
- I carry generations within my spirit.
- My voice is a gate through which revival flows.
- I rise and shine, for my light has come, and nations shall come to my rising *(*from *Isaiah 60 : 1 - 3, KJV)*.

Prayer

Father, thank You for calling me to be more than a woman. Thank You for making me a nation. Awaken the seed of nations within me. Give me the courage of Deborah, the faith of Mary, the strategy of Esther, and the strength of Sarah. Let my voice carry the sound of revival. May generations be blessed because I chose to arise. In Jesus' mighty name, Amen.

Prophetic Summary

This chapter reveals the identity of the woman as Heaven's nation-bearer. Your thoughts conceive vision, but your words give it form. You are not small; you are a divine government in motion. Speak, decree, and create, for the world is waiting for the sound of your rising.

Chapter 19

Arise and Shine

The Global Awakening of Daughters and Nations

"Arise, shine; for thy light is come, and the glory of the LORD is risen upon thee." **Isaiah 60 : 1 (KJV)**

This is the hour of awakening. Heaven is calling forth women from every corner of the earth - women who have cried, bled, served, prayed, and waited. This is the season when **the midnight cry becomes the morning light.**

Beloved daughter, you are not reading this by accident. You are reading because Heaven has marked you for manifestation. You have survived storms that others didn't because your light has an assignment.

The Lord is saying:

"Arise, Woman of Light for nations are waiting for your glow."

You have hidden long enough. You have healed long enough. You have stayed silent long enough. Now is the time to **arise**, to take your place in the army of women who will declare the glory of God to the ends of the earth.

When You Rise, Darkness Retreats

"For, behold, the darkness shall cover the earth, and gross darkness the people: but the LORD shall arise upon thee." **Isaiah 60 : 2 (KJV)**

The world is groaning under the weight of despair, fear, and confusion. But God's answer is not another program; it's a **woman with fire in her bones.**

Every time a woman rises in faith, darkness loses its grip over a generation. Your rising is not just personal; it's prophetic. Your "yes" to God is a torch passed to your children, your city, your church, and even your nation.

When you arise, your light announces that God is still on the throne. When you shine, you silence the lies that said you were finished.

You are Heaven's response to the darkness on earth.

From Weeping to Warring

"Weeping may endure for a night, but joy cometh in the morning." **Psalm 30 : 5 (KJV)**

Your tears were not wasted they were weapons. You wept through betrayal, loss, and waiting seasons, but the same tears that once fell in sorrow have watered your next season of joy.

It is time to turn your weeping into warring. Don't cry over what you've lost; fight for what remains. Stand up, woman of God, with your sword of the Spirit. Your pain has made you powerful.

No warrior shines until she has survived her own night. No woman truly glows until she has walked through her own darkness and found God still there.

A Global Call to Women of Light

This is not just about one woman; this is a movement: A movement of Deborahs rising to judge with wisdom, of Esthers standing before kings to save their people, of Hannahs birthing prophets through prayer, of Ruths walking in loyalty and legacy, of Marys carrying divine assignment, and of Rahabs opening the door to redemption.

Heaven is sounding the trumpet for a global awakening of women. **Arise, Daughters of Light!**

You are not too broken, too late, too lost, or too small. You are *the light*. You are *the voice*. You are *the generation God saw when He said, "Let there be light."*

The Mantle of Influence

"Nations shall come to thy light, and kings to the brightness of thy rising." **Isaiah 60 : 3 (KJV)**

When a woman arises in her purpose, kings notice. Influence is not sought; it's attracted by light.

You don't have to chase platforms; shine where you are, and Heaven will make your light visible. The anointing upon your life is magnetic. It draws those assigned to your voice.

Your home, your ministry, your career, your business, all are platforms of influence. Every time you speak in truth, encourage another, or stand in faith, your light reaches someone in darkness.

This is your Esther hour - not to hide your crown, but to use it to rescue others.

A Voice That Shapes Generations

There are women who will never step behind pulpits, but will shift atmospheres in boardrooms. There are mothers who will never write books, but will birth authors, prophets, and presidents through prayer. There are intercessors who may never be known by name, but whose words hold nations together.

Your voice is your assignment and it carries eternal weight.

"The Lord gave the word: great was the company of those that published it." **Psalm 68 : 11 (KJV)**

Heaven is looking for women who will echo His word until nations tremble and sons return home. You are one of them.

The Radiance of Restoration

Every time you forgive, you shine brighter. Every time you rise again, Heaven celebrates. Every time you declare hope instead of bitterness, your light expands.

The devil thought the betrayal would end you, but it only made you brighter. The pain that once tried to dim your fire has now become your oil.

Your restoration is not quiet; it glows. Your story will not end in ashes; it will end in light.

"For the LORD shall be unto thee an everlasting light, and thy God thy glory." **Isaiah 60 : 19 (KJV)**

For Reflection

1. Where is God calling you to arise in your home, ministry, or nation?
2. What light within you have you hidden that the world now needs to see?

Prophetic Declarations

• I arise and shine; my time has come.

• The glory of God is upon me; I am not hidden anymore.
• I am a voice to my generation and a light to my nation.
• Every darkness around me bows to the light of Christ within me.

- I am a torchbearer of revival, a carrier of glory, and a messenger of hope.

Prayer

Father, I thank You for awakening me in this hour. Let my light rise and never go dim. Use my life to ignite others, my voice to lift nations, and my story to release hope. I declare that my season of silence is over I arise to shine, to build, to heal, and to prophesy. Let Your glory rest upon me, and through me, light the world. In Jesus' mighty name, Amen.

Prophetic Summary: The Final Call

This is not the end; it is the *beginning of a movement*. From the ashes of pain, a generation of women is rising - radiant, healed, wise, and unstoppable.

The Spirit of the Lord says:

"You are My light in the earth. Nations will know Me through your rising."

So, arise, and when you do, remember: *You are a woman of light. You are a nation in motion. You are Heaven's answer to the darkness of this age.*

Arise, Woman of Light. The world is waiting for your shine.

A Word to Every Daughter Who Reads This Book

Daughter of light, You have walked through the pages of pain, promise, and prophecy. You have read of women who wept and then rose, and now the mantle has passed to you.

Heaven watches as you step into your divine assignment. The same God who spoke to Hannah in her anguish, who strengthened Esther before the throne, who gave Ruth a destiny among nations, is calling your name tonight.

You are no longer hidden. Your tears have been counted, your prayers have become incense before His throne. Every broken moment has been turned into oil, and the fire that once tested you now lights your path.

Rise, woman of valor. The world needs your voice. Your womb carries destiny; your words carry power. Your faith will open doors your fear once closed.

And when the enemy whispers, remind him that the light you carry cannot be dimmed. For you are the reflection of His glory - a daughter of prophecy, born for such a time as this.

Now walk. Walk into your nations. Walk into your businesses. Walk into your ministry, your home, your promise.

Arise, Woman of Light. Shine until the world sees Jesus in your strength, your gentleness, and your obedience.

May the oil of joy replace every tear. May your voice carry healing to generations. May your faith become fire wherever you go.

And may Heaven forever echo your story that in your rising, others found the courage to rise, too. **Amen.**

Psalm 46 (KJV)

God is our refuge and strength, a very present help in trouble.
Therefore will not we fear, though the earth be removed, and though the mountains be carried into the midst of the sea;
Though the waters thereof roar and be troubled, though the mountains shake with the swelling thereof. Selah.
There is a river, the streams whereof shall make glad the city of God, the holy place of the tabernacles of the most High.
God is in the midst of her; she shall not be moved: God shall help her, and that right early.
The heathen raged, the kingdoms were moved: he uttered his voice, the earth melted.
The Lord of hosts is with us; the God of Jacob is our refuge. Selah.
Come, behold the works of the Lord, what desolations he hath made in the earth.
He maketh wars to cease unto the end of the earth; he breaketh the bow, and cutteth the spear in sunder; he burneth the chariot in the fire.
Be still, and know that I am God: I will be exalted among the heathen, I will be exalted in the earth.
The Lord of hosts is with us; the God of Jacob is our refuge. Selah.

ABOUT THE AUTHOR

Dr. Prophetess Racheal Odoy is a prophetic voice to the nations - an anointed minister called to awaken destinies, heal hearts, and bring people into alignment with God's divine purpose. Her ministry carries a sharp prophetic mantle marked by wisdom, revelation, and transformation, inspiring people from all walks of life to rise into their calling.

A global motivational speaker and entrepreneur, she travels internationally proclaiming the message of faith, restoration, and hope. Through her teachings and writings, she empowers individuals to walk in their God-given identity and fulfill their heavenly assignment.

Dr. Odoy is the author of three other transformative titles: *You Need a Jonathan, I and My Seed Will Thrive,* and *You Have No Carbon Copy* - each carrying a prophetic message of destiny, faith, and divine alignment.

***

This book, *Arise, Woman of Light*, is the original work of Dr. Prophetess Racheal Odoy, drawn from her personal experiences, divine encounters, and spiritual insights. Any assistance provided in editing, formatting, or publication does not constitute shared authorship or ownership. All creative and intellectual rights remain solely with Dr. Prophetess Racheal Odoy.

www.ingramcontent.com/pod-product-compliance
Lightning Source LLC
Chambersburg PA
CBHW032056150426
43194CB00006B/544